No Matter What You're Going Through Count It
ALL JOY

No Matter What You're Going Through Count It
ALL JOY

MAURICE CARTER

atmosphere press

© 2025 Maurice Carter

Published by Atmosphere Press

Cover design by Dhiraj Navlakhe

No part of this book may be reproduced without permission from the author except in brief quotations and in reviews.

Atmospherepress.com

I thank God for all that He has done and all that He continues to do as I dedicate this book to my lovely wife, who was with me throughout the whole process. Thank God for the following individuals who were there for us to include: Dad and Mom, son and daughter, our family and members of our Church.

1

The Accident

In February 2016, my wife and I were involved in a head-on auto collision. We were on our way to bible study, as we do every Wednesday night before 7:00 pm, to get fed with the Word of God. This was a typical cool February night and our day was just normal.

We both worked. I was a Transportation Supervisor for a food Distribution Company, and my wife worked for a local Elementary School.

I have my CDL license (Commercial Driving License) and have been driving a tractor-trailer for approximately ten years: as a Transportation Manager for a Mexican company for six years; and Transportation Supervisor for a food distribution company for four years.

My current duties are supervising approximately twenty-five drivers to deliver food products to pizza places and coordinating a daily schedule for each driver. When drivers don't show up for work, I have to drive the tractor-trailer and deliver the product to the stores myself. All products must be delivered by hand cart, going up and down a ramp to be taken inside the stores.

This evening, around 6:30 pm, we were going through an

intersection with our light being green. Another driver was coming through on the other side of the intersection, and he was trying to make a left turn.

This vehicle I was driving was truly a blessing, as we needed another vehicle during this time. One of our church members had just purchased a brand new vehicle. I really didn't want to purchase this vehicle because it was a five-speed, and no one else in my family could drive a clutch. This vehicle was sold to us for $500, and the church member had also put another engine into this vehicle. This was truly a blessing during this time of our need. When I drove this vehicle, I had to move the seat up close because I had to push the clutch all the way to the floor to change gears. My knees were close to the dashboard because this was the only way to push in the clutch.

When we approached this intercession that night, all of a sudden we heard a loud "BOOM"! The other driver proceeded to make their turn and struck our car head-on. The impact was so hard that I received the most severe impact from this accident because he hit us on the driver's side. The windshield cracked right in front of our eyes, as it looked like a scene from a movie. I didn't realize how much damage was done to our vehicle. I knew that I was trapped on my side of the vehicle.

Everything in the car was thrown and scattered everywhere, but I was able to get a hold of my cell phone. I was able to make a call to our pastor to inform him that we were just involved in a head-on collision and would not make it to bible study tonight. I could hear our pastor mention to the other members that they needed to go into prayer for us.

The impact of the other vehicle hit us so hard; as the other car was moving so fast, the impact pushed our vehicle backward. What was this other driver thinking? Could he have assumed that he had an arrow or the right of way to make a left turn?

My wife and I were in so much pain! I looked over at my wife, and she, in turn, looked over at me. We both wanted to be sure that each of us was okay, but we were far from okay. One person's careless actions can impact and alter the course of other people's lives for a long time, sometimes permanently.

The pain I felt was like no other pain I had ever experienced before. I wasn't aware then, but the seat belt had crushed my wife's right shoulder, causing her bone to protrude through her shirt. The dashboard had crushed my left femur. My upper thigh and all the way down to my knee was crushed. I had no idea that this was the hardest bone in our body to break.

When the police came to the scene, the other driver came running over to the police officer. He stated that he had an arrow, and we came into his lane. I noticed that the police officer wasn't even paying any attention to this gentleman. He was more focused on trying to help us, as he saw that we were trapped in our vehicle. The police officer came to our aid, and asked if we were doing alright. He assured us that the ambulance was on the way, along with a fire truck, to assist in helping with our situation. I'm not sure how long it took before they arrived at the scene, but it sure seemed like a very long time.

The pain in my leg was so severe. I can only imagine the pain that my wife was experiencing in her shoulder. We started calling on the name of "Jesus" and began singing songs. I can't even explain, but we experienced such a powerful presence of God in that car. My wife and I started laughing so hard that we both had tears in our eyes. It seemed like the pain that we had wasn't so extreme as the presence of God was in our midst.

I'm not sure how long it took before the ambulance arrived, but the pain in my leg was starting to burn like it was on fire. Once the ambulance had arrived on the scene, many people were standing around watching. One of the gentlemen from the medic team came over and tried to open my door. To no avail; the door was crushed, and he couldn't open it. They were able to open the door for my wife and help her to get out on the passenger side. I also tried to open my door from the inside, but it wouldn't move at all. Some other medic team members came over to try to help open the door but realized this door was jammed. One of the medic team members mentioned that they needed to use the "Jaws of life" to pry open the door. They told me to cover myself, as this was going to shatter the windshield.

I know for me that this was something that I only saw in the movies, with someone being trapped in their vehicle. This was truly a reality for me, as they worked with the "Jaws of life" tool to pry me out. They had to cut the vehicle in several places just to get the door to open up. I could feel the pieces of glass being shattered on me, so I just closed my eyes and asked the Lord to keep me safe. Once they were able to get the driver-side door off, then they brought over a stretcher. It took about three of the medic team members to help get me out of the vehicle. They were trying not to pick me up because they saw the injury to my left leg. They had to turn me around to position me to get onto the stretcher. Once they grabbed me, I could feel a burning sensation in my left leg again.

I really wanted to shed some tears, but for some reason I was holding them back. They finally got me on the stretcher, and they had to raise me up to get me into the ambulance. Once they got me into the ambulance, I asked them where they were taking my wife. They weren't sure, especially since two separate ambulances arrived on the scene. There were two medic team members in the back with me. One of them cut my pant leg to take a look at the extent of my injuries.

This medic team member looked me in the eye and asked me for my name. I told him, and he had a look on his face that didn't look too good to me. He called me by my name and said he needed to raise me in the air to stretch my leg out. I didn't even question him to ask why he had to raise me up, but I just simply told him to do what he needed to do! They had this type of machine in the ambulance that can actually raise a person in the air. Once I was raised in the air, it took two of the medic team members to stretch out my leg. One of the medics mentioned to me that my leg was so crushed that it needed to be stretched out.

I never had my leg crushed before, so I had no idea why they had to do this. The pain in my leg from them stretching it out was so excruciating that I cried. It seemed like it took a few minutes to stretch out that leg, but it probably was a few seconds. Once they let me down, it felt like someone was taking their fist and hitting me in my leg. I asked the medic team member if he could give me some pain medicine. He told me they couldn't give me any pain relief until I arrived at the hospital. This same medic team member was working on that leg and trying to make it comfortable.

Once he realized this wasn't working, he looked me in the eye again and said, "I have to stretch your leg out again." This time I wanted to know the reason why he had to do this again. The first time was so painful, I needed to know the purpose of doing it a second time. The medic team member stated that my leg was so ruptured from the impact that they needed to try to prepare my leg for surgery. I assumed they were trying to save my leg, so the other medic was there to assist to raise me up again. They stretched out that leg again, and the pain was worse than the first time. Once they set me down, I was in so much pain that I asked again if they could give me some pain medicine. Of course, they wouldn't give me any until I arrived at the hospital to see the doctor.

2

At the Hospital

Upon arriving at the hospital, they rolled me into a room. The medic team member assured me that the doctor would take good care of me. I was still wondering what had happened to my wife and where they had taken her. After some time went by, two nurses came into the room where the medic team members had left me. They took my vital signs and assured me that the doctor would be in to see me soon.

In the meantime, I was able to make a call to my co-worker to inform him of what had just happened to my wife and me. I explained to him that we were just involved in a head-on collision, and he immediately asked, "Where are you?"

At the time, I wasn't aware of the hospital location the medic team members had taken me, so I asked one of the nurses. They told me the hospital's name, so I could relate this to my co-worker. He told me that he was on his way, and it amazed me that he arrived in such a short time. Once he entered my room, he asked me what happened. I just told him my wife and I were involved in a head-on collision. I was still waiting to see the doctor.

My co-worker saw that I was still in so much pain as he saw the tears running down from my eyes. I really appreciated his concern, and he went to find a doctor to come to look at me. As he was about to leave the room, I asked him to find out what hospital my wife was taken to.

A few minutes passed by, and the doctor came in to take a look at my leg... finally. I don't remember the doctor's name, but he asked my name and wanted me to answer a few questions. I told him that I needed some pain medicine to relieve the pain I was experiencing in my leg. He promised I would receive some pain medication, but he had to look at the leg first. He looked me in the eye, the same look I'd seen in the medic team member's eyes. The doctor stated that he had to do something before he could give me some pain medicine. At this moment, I just wanted him to do whatever he needed to do so that I could get some relief. He stated that he needed to raise me up and stretch my leg out. I informed him that the medics had already done this twice. He stated that my leg needed to be pulled out, so he asked the nurse to assist him as they stretched out that leg again (the third time). Once they stretched the leg out, the pain was worse than the first two times when it was done inside the Ambulance.

At this point, I was pleading with the doctor to give me some pain medication to relieve some of the excruciating pain. The doctor examined the leg again and still wasn't satisfied. He told me he needed to stretch the leg out again; this would be the fourth time the leg was stretched out. He proceeded with the nurse to raise me up, and they stretched the leg out one more time.

By this time, I was in so much pain the tears were flowing freely. The doctor did finally give me some pain medication. I don't know how long it took to relieve that pain, but I was so thankful for the relief.

I know the pain I had experienced was no comparison to the pain that Jesus had experienced as He went to the cross to die for my sin; when they put the nails in His hands and feet. Just knowing what Jesus went through for me, and the agony of Him being beaten all night before he went to the cross. This was truly God's love for me, to have His only begotten Son, "Jesus Christ," to take the penalty that I deserved, which is death. Even though God's son didn't commit any sin, He became sin on my behalf. What an awesome God we serve, to have His only Son, to take on my sin debt. When I realized what Jesus went through on my behalf, I just started rejoicing to know that He was in control of my current situation.

So, while I was still in the waiting room after receiving that pain medication, my co-worker returned. He found out my wife was delivered to the same Hospital in another room. Once he gave me that news, I was relieved to know where my wife was taken and wanted to know what was being done to her right shoulder. The more I engaged in a conversation with my co-worker, I was starting to drift off to sleep. I heard him mention that he would inform my Supervisor of my current situation.

Once he left, after spending some time with me, my son arrived with his girlfriend to check on us. They had already visited my wife, and my son was really concerned about what would be done about our situation. My son left the room but came back to tell me that a doctor had given my wife some pain medication to relieve the pain in her shoulder. The doctor came back to visit me again while my son was there with me. He stated that they would keep me overnight and prepare me for surgery first thing in the morning.

I don't remember when, but they rolled me to a room to get me situated. The next morning I was awakened with my wife standing over me, along with my son and daughter. This was the first time I had seen my wife since they took her away in the other ambulance. My wife told me that she was sent home last night with some pain medication, as her bone was sticking out on her right shoulder.

I was about to ask her what else was done when the surgeon who was going to perform my surgery came into the room to speak to us. He introduced himself and then went on to explain the purpose of why he was there. He mentioned that my left leg was broken in several places, and my femur had been shattered. He stated that he would have to put some rods in my leg to hold it together, and the surgery would take several hours.

After explaining to my family and me about the process of what was going to be done, he then asked if anyone had any questions. My wife had several questions about the surgery, and she also mentioned her shoulder to the doctor. He took a look at her shoulder, and she told him that she was sent home with just some pain medication. The doctor was quite shocked, but he told her to call his office the next day to set up an appointment to schedule surgery for her as well. My children also had some questions to ask the doctor, and he asked me if I had any questions. I told the doctor I just wanted to know one thing, "Do you know God?"

The doctor said, "I have a Christian family here, so would it be okay if I prayed for you and your family?" Just hearing him say that gave me such peace, as I sensed God's presence was in that room.

At that very moment, I knew that God had sent this Christian doctor to perform the surgery on my leg and my wife's surgery on her shoulder. This doctor took the time to pray for us, and for God to direct him to do the surgery, so that God's will be done. This was such a powerful experience for our children to witness how God was moving in the midst of our situation. It's truly a blessing to see how God was working things out for His good pleasure, as He sent this doctor to perform these major surgeries on my leg and to place my wife's shoulder back in place as well. Before the doctor departed the room and prayed for us, he mentioned that some nurses would be coming to take me to the room to prepare me for surgery.

I could see the peace of God all over my wife, but my children still had some fear of me going through this major surgery. I reminded my children of a familiar passage of scripture that they had remembered in the book of Proverbs 3:5-6. "Trust in the Lord with all your heart, and lean not on your own understanding. In all your ways acknowledge Him, and He will direct your path."

I wanted them to know that God was directing the eyes and the hands of this doctor, whom God had chosen to perform this major surgery on my leg. The nurses arrived to take me away to the surgery room. I have to admit that I wasn't afraid of what was about to take place. I knew that God was in control, and He reminds us in His word 1 Peter 5:7, "Cast all our cares upon Him, as He cares for us."

Not only did God protect us in this accident, but He was also ordering our steps through each phase of placing the right people in our path. The surgery did take a few hours before it was complete. I can only imagine what my wife and children were going through in the midst of their waiting. After the surgery was done, the surgeon went to inform my family that everything had gone well. I was still in the recovery stage and still under heavy medication. Once I was able to comprehend, I looked up and saw my wife, along with my children, standing there with the doctor.

The doctor explained all that was done during the surgery. He mentioned that he had to put three rods in my leg to keep it stable. The femur was shattered from my hip all the way down to my knee. He mentioned that I would be in the Hospital for a few days. I would need some help to get in and out of bed. He also stated that I would have to go through physical therapy to help me learn how to walk again. I would also have to use a walker to help me walk in the next few weeks.

After the doctor explained everything that happened and what would occur while in the hospital, he said I would have some pads on my legs to help prevent blood clots. The doctor was still talking, and I started to feel some more pain in that leg. The nurse came in to give me some Percocet medicine, which, at the time, took away that pain in just a few minutes. I didn't realize it at the time, but I was allergic to this medication. This medication was really strong, but it took away the pain right away. My back was starting to feel like I needed to scratch it, along with my legs that were starting to turn red due to scratching them.

That night, I was awakened by a nurse who came in to check on me. I heard a beeping sound from the machine. I didn't know why this machine was making this noise. This nurse was an older gentleman who also noticed the beeping sound and saw me with sweat on my forehead. I felt lightheaded and dehydrated, so he checked my vital signs. After checking my vital signs, the nurse left the room. I started to sweat even more, so I pressed the button to call for a nurse. Once another nurse arrived and saw me sweating, she asked me why I didn't call a nurse sooner. Right then, my heart started beeping faster than normal. This nurse immediately called in the head nurse as she realized I didn't look well. The head nurse was concerned about me having an anxiety attack or maybe a stroke. They brought in a heart scanner to make sure I wasn't having a heart attack, especially since my heart was racing so fast. It actually turned out that I was dehydrated because the machine had run out of fluids. Praise God that everything was checked out to be fine with me not having a stroke or heart attack because my heart was racing faster than normal. They replaced the fluid in the machine, which also stopped the beeping noise. Once the fluid started to flow, I started to calm down without sweating a lot.

The head nurse asked me again why I had waited so long to call in a nurse. I told her that another nurse had come in to check on me and checked my vital signs, and then he left. I wanted to say something more out of my flesh, but I knew what I wanted to say wouldn't have been nice. The head nurse asked me another question, but instead of answering her question, I asked her if she knew Jesus, and she then paused for a moment. She actually had some tears start flowing down her face. She said that she knew Jesus and even went to Church. This was truly through the power of the Holy Spirit, as I told her that God knows what she's going through. I asked her if I could pray for her, and before she gave me an answer, I just started praying for her as the holy spirit gave me the words to pray. After I finished praying for her, she was filled with joy and tears.

She then asked me, "How can you pray for me in your condition when I should be praying for you?"

I told her that it wasn't me, but the Christ that lives in me. I told her that no matter what we're going through, we must understand that God has a purpose for us to draw nearer to Him. That's why we must keep our eyes fixed on Jesus, the author and finisher of our faith. Another nurse standing there just witnessed the powerful presence of God in that room.

I told them that God loves them and His desire is for them to draw closer to God by coming to know His Son, Jesus Christ. They both appreciated what was said and checked my vital signs again. They both left with the reassured confidence that I was doing okay. I was able to get a good night's rest, even though I had some pain again in my leg throughout the night.

The next day, some visitors came in from our church to check on me. I was glad to see some of the church members from the body of Christ. I explained to them the ordeal my wife and I went through from the accident. These members of our church were at bible study when this accident happened that night. They heard the Pastor tell them that they needed to go into prayer for some members of our church. They didn't know what we had experienced, but I told them how this gentleman had tried to make a left turn in our lane. It was mentioned to them that he hit us so hard on my side that I was trapped in the vehicle. I told them that we were in so much pain during that night that we could only call on the name of "Jesus." It was truly a powerful experience as we felt the presence of God in our midst, even though we were in so much pain that we started laughing and singing songs to keep our minds off the pain we were experiencing. They were overjoyed that God had protected us through the midst of this tragic accident. They didn't stay long, but they prayed with me and reminded me that God loves us. I really appreciated these members coming by to pray because, in these crises, you need the members of the body of Christ to be on your side.

In reality, we had no idea what challenges we would face in the next few months. The God of all creation already knew what we were about to face. That same day, my wife came to see me with her arm in a sling. She told me she had met with the doctor who did my surgery and scheduled surgery on her shoulder. After we discussed the time of her surgery, we also decided that we needed to contact a lawyer about our accident. Since this was our first time contacting a lawyer and since this was our first accident, we decided to contact a familiar lawyer. We looked up a lawyer on our phone and also decided to contact this lawyer that afternoon. This lawyer took our information over the phone and made an appointment to have someone visit us the next day.

The next day, a representative from the lawyer's office visited us at the hospital. We didn't know what to expect, but this representative came prepared to start on our case. He asked us a lot of questions, but he also had some documents for us to sign to start things rolling on our case. We normally take the time to pray before we make a decision, but we decided to sign the paperwork. We just assumed that this was a good lawyer to represent us. After discussing what happened, we signed the documents, and he said he would be in touch with us. After the representative from the lawyer's office left, my wife and I discussed what we had just done. I'm not sure what was going on in my wife's mind, but in my mind, I thought that we were going to get paid. I thought about some of the advertisements on TV from this law firm advertisement, from some of his clients that received hundreds of thousands of dollars for their cases. My mind was far away from asking "The Lord" for clear directions. Proverbs 16:9 "A man's heart plans his ways, but the Lord directs his steps."

It's so easy in life to look at how we make plans first and then go to God second or third or just think that we know what's best. We think we know better than God, so we decided to move forward with this lawyer's team. Meanwhile, as I was still going through that pain in my leg, the most challenging thing occurred when the physical therapy team came in to help me walk. I don't remember my childhood trying to walk, but this was truly painful trying to even get out of bed. They knew what they were doing to help me, so I cooperated with them as they got me out of bed. When I saw that they had one of those walkers that old people use, I said that this was for older people to help them walk. Of course, they explained to me that this was what I needed in order for them to help me in the beginning stages of walking again.

When I finally got out of the bed and tried to stand up on my one leg, it was truly a great challenge. They didn't want me to put all the pressure on one leg; they helped me by standing me up and putting pressure on the other leg. I gave thanks for the therapists that were helping me; the lady was gentle, but the gentleman had no sense of sympathy for me at all. He wanted me to get up and walk as if I hadn't undergone surgery. I was starting to get a little frustrated with him, but I had to accept the fact that he was trying to encourage me and not have pity for me. They both took their time to help me as I finally stood up with that walker. That first step on that left leg was truly a challenge, so they put a waistband on my waist so I wouldn't lose my balance.

I had to take one step at a time, which was truly painful. I had never had rods put in my leg before, but it felt like sharp pains running through my legs. I wasn't sure if it was the rods in my leg or just because standing up with all that pressure on the leg was so painful. They kept encouraging me that I could do it. I've experienced some challenging things in my life, but this was truly at the top of the list. It took them a few minutes to get me into the hallway, but I finally made it there with their help. After we took a few steps down the hallway, I started to sweat and got tired. In my mind, I thought that this wouldn't be a problem taking a few steps.

It was the enemy playing tricks on my mind, making me think I would never run or walk normally again. After all, I was in good shape, as I was a runner, and enjoyed working out.

The therapists saw that I was really tired, so they helped me get back into the room and assisted me in getting back into bed. They told me I had done a wonderful job for the first time. I told them I really appreciated them and thanked God for their patience in working with me. I needed some pain medicine because I was in so much pain from that walking exercise. I was truly exhausted and wanted to get some relief from the pain and go to sleep. The nurses came in to check on me. They saw that I was exhausted and asked if I needed anything, so they gave me some pain medicine to relieve it.

After getting some rest, I was awakened by my wife, who was standing over me with smiles all over her face. The first thing I said was, "What are you doing here?" She was still experiencing that pain in the right shoulder from the accident. She was more concerned about me, but yet she also needed to have surgery on her right shoulder. I'm not sure who the doctor was that saw my wife that night, but she should have never been sent home with that right shoulder like it was. They should have at least repaired her shoulder to relieve some of the pain instead of sending her home with just some pain medicine. Apparently, God knew, at the time, who needed to do the surgery to repair my wife's shoulder.

We may not know why things happen the way they do in our lives, but we must trust God and know that he knows what's best for us. God is truly all-loving, merciful and just in all His ways. For His Word says in Isaiah 55:8–9, "For my thoughts are not your thoughts, and my ways are not your ways, for high as the heavens are above the earth, so are my ways higher than your ways."

As I spoke to my wife about her shoulder, she mentioned that she had already called the doctor to schedule an appointment for her surgery. When she told me this, in my mind, I wanted to be there to support my wife. This was a little frustrating for me, as I couldn't be there for her, yet she was there for my surgery. What a wonderful wife to have, as she had put her needs behind her to be there for me. I explained that I wanted to be there for her surgery, but she understood my condition and that it was best to keep her in prayer. We then began to pray together, asking for God to guide the hands of the doctor so that God's plan would be fulfilled to do an awesome surgery on my wife's shoulder. The doctor did perform the surgery on my wife's right shoulder while I was still at the hospital during my recovery. They didn't have to keep her overnight, but they kept her to observe her for a few hours. After her recovery, she was able to go home with a sling on her right shoulder. Both of our children were there with her, and they informed me that everything went well. I just started praising God for using the doctor to perform both of our major surgeries.

God is truly an awesome God, as He gets all the praise and all the glory for all that He has done. This was now the fifth day that I was in the hospital and the third day that I had been doing physical therapy. It was truly a blessing that God sent the same people to work with me, as I asked God to give them the patience to work with me. I kept getting frustrated because I wanted to hurry up the process. I had to get it in my mind that this would take some time; even though this accident happened in one night, trying to walk with those rods in my leg would take a few months. On my sixth day in the hospital and my last day of doing physical therapy, the doctor came in for his last visit.

My doctor stated that I would be released that day. He mentioned that I would have to follow up with an in-house physical therapist to come to my house. My wife and children came to the hospital to take me home that day. Seeing them, especially my wife, with that sling on her right shoulder was truly a blessing. The two physical therapists were there to help me get into the chair and roll me out to the car. I had built up a good relationship with them both, especially talking about the goodness of God and how they helped me so much. I was given some instructions that the doctor gave me, especially since I had to give myself a shot in my leg every day for thirty days. This was to prevent blood clots that could occur after having surgery. I asked the Lord to give me strength, as I had no idea how challenging getting me into the car would be. I don't remember how long it took, but it took quite a while to get that leg situated into the car, but we finally managed.

3

Facing Challenges at Home

Once I arrived home, we parked the car in the garage. A second challenge was getting me out of the car, as my son was there to help me. Those rods in my leg were like someone sticking needles down my side as they tried to move me out of the car. My son finally helped me to get into the house, and he also helped me to get into bed. It was truly a blessing that years ago, when we purchased this house, the main bedroom was on the first floor. Once I came out of the garage, this door was to enter through the kitchen, and our bedroom was next to the kitchen. I didn't have to go up any steps, which would have been a great challenge at that time. It is truly a blessing that God knew when we purchased this home that we needed to have our bedroom on the first floor. Once I got settled in, I was ready for some pain medicine to go right to sleep. I was truly exhausted as my energy was drained from coming from the hospital to our home. Once I received some good rest that day, I was flooded with phone calls to check to see how we were doing.

At this time, my parents were living in Baltimore, and they were concerned for my wife and me. I got a call from my dad that brought tears to my eyes. My dad wasn't a man of compassion, but I could hear the concerns from our conversation. He wanted to know how I was doing physically, and he also wanted to know how I was doing financially. He told me that he had purchased a plane ticket to send my mother down for a few weeks to help take care of us. I was just so overwhelmed as I just burst into tears.

My father stated that this was a time that we needed some help, so that's why he was going to send my mother to help take care of us. This was truly a blessing from the Lord because my wife couldn't do much with her right arm still in a sling.

My wife is also right-handed, so she had to try to help herself and me with her left arm. My wife and I were now having some time to be alone, and especially since I couldn't get out of bed as much, all the responsibility was now on my wife. As this was the second day of being home, I had mentioned to my wife that I needed to take a shower. I knew it would be a great challenge for me to get out of the bed, so I had to wait for my son to come over to help me. The day prior, with her one arm, my wife had washed me while I was in bed. My son helped me get out of bed, and I had to use my walker to walk to the bathroom. My son stepped out of the room, and my wife helped me to take off my clothes.

It's truly amazing how in life, we take for granted that we can do things for ourselves. This was a time I couldn't do for myself, and I felt helpless. The next greatest challenge was to try to help me to step into the shower to wash. I tried using the walker, but it only got in the way. I was now truly exhausted by just trying to get into the shower to wash myself. I truly thank God for sending me a wife who has compassion. She saw that I was getting frustrated, and I told her that we needed to do this another time. I do remember asking God to give me strength, but this was a task that just took all my strength. I know I wanted to take a shower, but I just told my wife that we'd have to do this another time. My wife just helped me put my clothes back on and helped me to get back into bed.

My daughter came over that day, and she noticed that I needed to shave. At this time, I was using what is called the Magic Shave, which had a terrible smell. My daughter said that she wanted to help and shave me. She got what I needed, made up the cream and got a towel under me. She actually took the time and shaved me that day, which was truly a blessing to see how our children were willing to do whatever it took to help us out. After she finished, she washed my face with a hot towel and then put some lotion on my face. I told her this reminded me of what she and her cousin would do for their Grandfather. They used to do this to my father when they were around six or seven years old. We laughed about that and had a good time at that moment.

After my daughter had cleaned up everything, I was ready to take a nap as the pain was starting to settle in on my leg. I took some pain medicine, and I also had to give myself a shot (a needle) in my leg to help prevent blood clots. During my time resting, my wife could use that one arm to do some cleaning around the house. She also took the time to cook dinner, preparing a good meal for us.

As I awakened that afternoon, my wife came into the room and asked how I was feeling. I told her I wasn't doing well and asked her what she was doing. That's when she told me that she was cooking and cleaning the house. I just smiled! I was just thankful that God had sent me a help mate that was willing to take care of all our needs around the house despite her condition. I realized that it was only by God's grace that my wife was able to help us both in our time of need. Paul says in the book of Philippians 2:3-4, "Let nothing be done through selfish ambition or conceit, but in lowliness of mind, let each esteem others better than himself. But let each of you look out not only for his own interests, but also for the interests of others."

I truly saw the love of Christ working in and through my

wife, but it is God who works in us to will and to do for His good purpose. In spite of my challenges, as I couldn't do much to help my wife. I knew that she was also experiencing some pain and challenges, but she was looking beyond her own needs. This is truly the love of Christ, and I just wanted to say, "Lord, I thank You for my wife."

That evening, my son came over and asked what needed to be done on the outside of the house. I asked him if he could cut and trim the grass. He knew how to cut the grass, but he wasn't too familiar with trimming. He went out and cut the front and back yard. This was truly a blessing! He worked all day and took some time to take care of the yard for us. After finishing up cutting the yard, he also took some time out to wash both of our cars. I didn't even ask him to do this, but he took it upon himself. I was thanking God for both of our children, who took time out of their busy schedules to come and help us out around the house in our time of need.

That evening, I told my wife that I wanted to try to take a shower. She prepared all that I needed in the bathroom and also helped me to get ready for my shower. This was such a great challenge, as I didn't know how to get into the shower without my walker. Here we go, my wife with that one arm and trying to help me step into that shower. It was truly a struggle, but we managed, and I was in so much pain. Once I got into the shower, my wife took the time to wash the parts of my body that I couldn't get to. I wasn't able to bend down, so with her one arm, she was there to take care of those needs. I made a comment as she was washing my legs and feet. We just laughed about that moment as I told her that it's amazing how we take these little things for granted. Not being able to wash myself, I had to depend on my wife to wash my body.

We should never take any day for granted, as we are awakened by our God each day. The word of God reminds us that His mercies are new every morning, and great is His faithfulness.

Most people don't even take the time to give thanks for a brand new day. Most people who claim to be a follower of Christ don't take the time to spend with Him and his Word. I know for me, I need His Word daily, just as I need to nourish my body with natural food. Our inner man needs to be nourished with the Word of God so that we may grow in the likeness of Christ. 1 Peter 2:2 reminds us, "As newborn babies, desire the sincere milk of the word that you may grow thereby."

I know that all my wife and I have gone through and continue to go through; we couldn't even endure this without the strength of Christ. Paul reminds us in Philippians 4:13, "We can do all things through Christ who strengthens us."

The next day came, and I was awakened to give thanks and to start this brand new day in God's Holy Word. This was also truly a blessing for my wife and me to spend quality time together in prayer, along with our morning devotion. I just saw how God was strengthening our marriage relationship, as we had no other choice but to spend that quality time together. My wife always tells me that I don't talk or communicate enough, but we were having such great conversations talking about the Lord. We started talking about our children and how we see God working in their lives. Our prayers are always that our children draw closer to the Lord, spend time in His word more each day, have a more intimate relationship with our creator, and attend Church.

After our morning devotion and spending some time talking, my wife went to prepare some breakfast for us. She also spent some time cleaning the house. That morning, I also received a call from the doctor, who wanted to check in on me. He was also calling to schedule a physical therapist to visit our home twice a week. This person would come out and help me to learn how to walk on that left leg. I also received a call from my mother that afternoon, stating that my father had purchased a flight ticket for her to come down to help us in our time of need. I was, once again, praising God for orchestrating every detail!

This load was just too much for my wife, as she also was experiencing pain in her right shoulder. She still had to wear a sling and was doing everything with that left arm. I was amazed that she was right-handed but doing everything around the house with her left arm. That day, we also received a call from my wife's school that they wanted to bring over some food for us. Some of her co-workers gathered together and prepared some meals for us. This was truly a blessing to take the load off my wife to cook. They brought the food over that afternoon, but I didn't see them come in. Our church family had also called to check up on us, and they also wanted to bring over some food. I thank God for providing for us, especially to give my wife some relief from having to cook and take care of me.

We have a good relationship with our church family, and I can honestly say that they are family. They not only provided us with food, but their prayers were constant, with someone always calling from the church to see what we needed. Our pastor also called to check on us and took some time to pray with us. This is truly the body of Christ, helping others in their time of need. We didn't realize how much we needed this at the time, but I know for me that I really needed the prayers of the saints. So much was going through my mind, just thinking if I would be able to walk or run again. Would I ever be able to go back to work driving a tractor-trailer?

I didn't share with my wife what was going through my mind at this time, but I was feeling lonely. I truly had more time to spend with God, reading His word and praying. I started thinking about how long I would be out of work. All these thoughts were playing in my mind, which can be a heavy load on oneself at this particular time. I wasn't sure how my wife felt or what was going through her mind. I didn't realize it at the time, but my wife was also concerned about how we would continue to pay our bills since I wasn't able to work.

It's amazing that we all go through our own personal trials, and that's when the enemy tries to come against us. These are times when we must encourage one another and share what's on our minds.

I remember lying in bed while reading about David's life. The time when Saul was pursuing him and David hid himself in the cave. David wasn't sure why Saul was so adamant about killing him. David was tired of running from Saul, and he was getting weary. Since David was a warrior, he was aware of the enemy, but Saul wasn't an enemy. Saul, at the time, was the king. David respected his position as a king. During this time of running and hiding, David had to encourage himself. He didn't feel sorry for himself, and I had to do the same. I knew God loved me and that he wouldn't put any more on me than I couldn't bear.

I was starting to feel quite lonely, and a little frustrated, but God's words reminded me, in 1 Peter 5:7, "Cast all of my cares upon Him because He cares for us." It's truly a blessing to know that God loves us so much that he sent his only begotten son, "Jesus Christ," to die on the cross for our sins. It is God who works in us, to will and to do for his good purpose. I had to remind myself that what I was going through was no comparison to what Jesus went through to redeem us (buy back) and pay a ransom for our sins. Mark 10:45 says from the words of Jesus, "For even the Son of man did not come to be served, but to serve and to give His life as a ransom for many."

The evening after I had spent some time in God's word, my wife fixed us a plate to eat. We talked that evening, and I shared with her some of the things that I was struggling with. After watching some TV and dozing off to rest, I had a rough night as I kept tossing and turning because of the pain in my leg. The doctor had prescribed some Percocet medicine, and that night I was scratching all night long as my back and legs were itching so much. The pain had gone down some after I took the medicine, but I just couldn't stop scratching my back and legs. I asked my wife to look at my back, and it looked like someone had taken a whip to it.

I didn't realize at the time that I was allergic to Percocet medicine. It truly helped me with the pain, but it caused me to stay up all night scratching. The next day I called the doctor, and he told me in the meantime to take some extra-strength Tylenol for the pain. My wife had to go out to get the prescription, but she didn't want to leave me home alone. I told her I would be okay, but she called our son to pick up the medicine from the pharmacy instead.

4

Do We Trust God to Meet All Our Needs?

We also received some more food that day from my wife's co-workers. This was truly a blessing. I also had an interesting phone call from my employer that day. They asked me how I was doing and how my wife was doing. I told them that she was doing well. They also asked me how long I thought I would be off work. I told him I had no idea, especially since I still had to undergo some therapy. They asked because I would be receiving my last paycheck from them this coming Friday. This job didn't have any long-term or short-term disability. The last check would be from my last week of sick leave that I didn't use.

We got paid weekly, so they asked me what I would do after this week. I told him that I worked for him, so I had no idea how I would get paid after this week. He also asked me if my wife was getting paid, with her being off as well. I told him that as of the next week, her long-term disability would be starting. He said he hoped I would get better and would be back in touch with me soon, and then ended the call with me. I shared the news with my wife, and she asked me what we were going to do with no money coming in. I told her that we were going to trust God! He knows our needs. The word of God says in Philippians 4:19, "He will supply all of my needs according to his riches and glory in Christ Jesus."

I could see on my wife's face that she was worried and had some concerns. My job stated that I would not be getting a paycheck from them next week, and my wife's pay would be reduced. This was truly a situation where we just had to trust God for all of our needs. I told my wife that God has allowed this to happen for His glory. I didn't know how our needs were going to be met, but I did know that we serve a God that's faithful to His Word. I started reading and proclaiming His Word, but the enemy was already trying to put doubt in my mind. I had some concerns about how we were going to pay our mortgage, not being able to make our car payment, along with how our insurance and other obligations were going to be paid. All these thoughts were playing in my mind, but I had to take every thought captive and make it obedient to Christ Jesus.

I had to remind myself that God is faithful, just, and merciful, all-loving and all-powerful in all His ways. For we walk by faith and not by sight. That evening, I also received a call from my mother to inform me that she would be arriving the next day. Someone will have to go to the airport to pick her up. My son was going to be off that day, so we called him and had him go to pick up his grandmother from the airport.

I was speaking to my father that evening, and he asked me how I was doing. He also asked me if I needed anything. I wanted to tell him that I needed some money at that time, but I allowed my pride to get in the way of not asking him to send me some money. I told him that we would be okay and that we were just glad to be alive. He also stated that he thanked God for that as well. I asked him if he would be okay without his wife for a week or two. He stated that we needed her more than he did at this particular time. After he said that, I got a little teary-eyed and thanked him. I told him I loved him, and then our conversation ended.

I had another rough night, as the new medicine wasn't working to take away the pain soon enough. I remembered the doctor saying I could take the new medicine he prescribed, along with some extra strength Tylenol. Each night was a challenge, trying to get comfortable on that leg with the rods inside.

The next day my son picked up my mother from the airport, and they arrived safely at our home. It was truly a blessing to see my mother and for her to take some time to come down and help us in our time of need. It's amazing how my mom got settled in and immediately went straight to the kitchen and started preparing dinner for us.

I can honestly say there's nothing like mom's cooking, as she fixed a good meal that evening. This was also a blessing for my wife and a relief for her, even though we had received some meals from her school. The next day, as we were awakened by God's appointed time, I still had a struggle trying to rest that night.

There was a knock at our door, as this was the physical therapist arriving for my first in-house appointment. I had already eaten some breakfast, and I had already taken my pain medicine that morning. My wife brought her to our room, so she introduced herself and gave us her background about what she does. I felt comfortable about her background and how she had helped other patients as well. She then asked me a few questions and also wanted to know if I had a goal of when to get better. I don't recall exactly what I said, but I told her that it was in the hands of God to help me walk again. I saw the smile on her face, and she also agreed that it was in God's timing.

After we finished talking, she then went straight into doing some physical exercise. These exercises weren't too bad, and she wanted to see where to start and how much pain I could take from moving my legs up and down. In just those few moments, I saw that she knew exactly what she was doing as she pulled out this chart to measure my legs after doing some exercises. I had some pads around both of my legs, as this was to prevent me from getting blood clots.

The therapist took both of the pads off so that she could see how far I could move both of my legs. She pulled out a ruler as she had to measure both of my legs to see how far the progress would be as she took the leg measurements. I started moving that one leg motion, and she called it as five percent. The therapist's goal was to get my leg at about forty or fifty percent motion before she finished with me.

After we were finished with my exercise, she asked if I had any more questions about what was done today. I didn't have any questions to ask, but my wife had a few things that she wanted to know. She answered her questions, and then she stated that today was a light day for her first time doing physical therapy with me. Her next schedule for coming out to do physical therapy would be every Tuesday and Thursday. It was also mentioned that she would fill in some Fridays as well. Before she departed, she reminded me to do all the exercises we went over from a sheet she had given me to do daily.

After she left, it seemed like we didn't do much, but I was tired. I told my wife I needed some rest, as these exercises wore me out. I had a good nap and was awakened refreshed.

My mom came into the room to check on me and also wanted to know if I wanted something to eat. I told her that all I needed was a sandwich, and I asked her where my wife was. She told me that she had gone out to see her doctor. I had forgotten that she had to follow up with the same doctor that did my surgery.

My mom came in with the sandwich, and I was able to share with her about our accident. I stated how I was crushed on the driver's side and all the excruciating pain we were experiencing. My mom said that she didn't want to hear any more about our accident, but she thanked God that we were alive. I immediately noticed that this was a sensitive moment for my mom, so I didn't mention any more about our accident to her. Mom then left the room.

I started reading God's word in the old testament. I normally do a daily devotion each morning to start my day, spending quality time in God's word. I just can't imagine one who has a relationship with God through Jesus Christ, and how they can go daily without being nourished with the word of God. In Matthew 4:4, Jesus says, "Man shall not live by bread alone, but by every word that proceeds out of the mouth of God."

At this point in time, Jesus was fasting and was being tempted by the devil. I believe we must have a daily diet of God's Word in order for a person to grow spiritually. I believe it's important that we meditate on His Word day and night. I remember reading about Joshua in the old testament when he had to take on the assignment of leading God's people to the land of Canaan. The people, the children of Israel, were familiar with God speaking to His servant Moses.

Unfortunately, Moses died and was no longer with them going into the land that God had promised them. Joshua now had to listen not only to God's voice but also to the people he had to lead. Truly Joshua had a tremendous responsibility of crowding out the voices of the people and to listen to God's voice only. God told him in Joshua 1:8, "This Book of the Law shall not depart from your mouth, but you shall meditate in it day and night, that you may observe to do according to all that is written in it, for then you will make your way prosperous and have good success."

As God told Joshua to be strong and of good courage, do not be afraid, nor be dismayed, for the Lord your God is with you wherever you go. What a blessing to know that as God was with the old testament saints, He's truly with us as new testament Saints. As a follower of Jesus Christ, I have the Father, the Son, and the Holy Spirit dwelling in me. This is awesome to know that I have the trinity living on inside of me. That's why it's important for me to spend daily time with God in His Word.

In order for me to know Him and hear from Him, spending quality time reading His Word must be a priority for me. I couldn't imagine going through this accident on my own strength or ability. I also couldn't imagine Joshua trying to lead all of God's people to a place he's never been before without the guidance of God's word. It was through Moses that Joshua had the experience of seeing how Moses heard from God and how the people responded. The people not only grumbled, but they also complained as well. Joshua was able to witness that this grumbling and complaining wasn't against Moses, but against God.

We even see this today, of how so many people grumble and complain about many issues they face. After spending some time with God in His word, my wife arrived back from her appointment with the doctor. She looked really tired, as if some rest was needed due to her going over some physical exercise with the doctor. My wife had to continue doing her exercises at home, along with wearing a sling around her shoulder. I thought she was going to get some rest, but she went to help my mom clean around the house. That day we also had some visitors from my wife's job, as they came to see how we were doing. They mentioned that many people were praying for our recovery at her school, and they also brought over some food for us to eat. This was truly a blessing to hear that others were praying on our behalf, along with the food that was brought over. They stayed a little while talking to my wife, but I stayed in the other room.

After they left, my wife came into the room with me, and we both took a nap together. I was surprised to see my wife come to take a nap with me because she normally doesn't do this. I can only say that she was tired from her visit to the doctor. That evening, my mom fixed another great meal for us. I told her that I needed to get well, so I could start exercising. I was a runner, and I really enjoyed exercising, so being that I wasn't able to do this was still frustrating for me. I remember one year I was training to run a 10k run, which is about 5.6 miles. I asked my son and his friend to run this event with me. They agreed, and we all started training for about two and a half months. I made sure that they drank plenty of water, and I told them that they needed to change their diet. It was truly a blessing to work out with my son and his friend as God drew us closer.

After training with them and arriving on the day of the event, I informed them that this was not a sprint race and prayed with them. As we started the run, I informed them they needed to pace themselves. They both took off like jackrabbits, and I started pacing myself, knowing I would catch up with them. We had several hills to run up, so after about the fourth or fifth hill; I was able to catch up with them. I just passed right by them as I still had the same pace. They were walking and breathing very hard, but we all finished the run as they came in behind me. I was truly proud of them both that they completed this run, even though they started out running too fast. I reminded them that it's not how you start the race, but how you finish.

Those encouraging words were brought back to my memory to remind me that one day I will be able to run again. I reminded my wife of this event and told her that God would give me the strength and ability to run again. In the meantime, I still had to do my daily exercise with my leg in the bed. The therapist left me with a rope to pull up and down on my leg, so I wouldn't get cramps. This was also to help me not to build up blood clots because I still had to give myself a shot (a needle) each morning.

The next day, my therapist arrived early in the morning. She did call before she came to make sure that I was awake and dressed for her arrival. She came in with a mindset to be ready for a good workout. The first thing she did was to measure my leg, which was still at five percent. We did some leg exercises on the bed, and then she told me it was time to walk around the house. I had this walker to help me so that I wouldn't fall. We went into our living room, and then she told me to sit in a chair. She took the leg with the rods in and tried to raise it up. I was in so much pain, but I tried to hold it in. She raised the leg several times, and then she measured my leg again. I couldn't believe it was at ten percent, by her moving my leg up and down. After we finished, she said that she was proud of me and then she asked if I was ever in the military. I told her that I was in the army, and she stated that I was able to endure much pain.

After she left and I was sitting in the living room, I wanted to sit up for a while. That afternoon I received a visit from two of my co-workers from my current employer. It was a pleasure seeing them as they came to check up on me and to see how I was doing. There was one gentleman who came down from Toledo, Ohio. We talked about the job and what had happened to my wife and me in the accident. I had some pictures of the accident to show them, and they hadn't realized how severe this accident was we were involved in. I was sharing with them that it was God that brought us through and allowed us to be alive to testify to His goodness. After listening about our situation, they gave thanks to God, as they also were thankful that we were alive as well.

At this moment of speaking to these co-workers, I realized that this was an opportunity to share how the peace of God was upon us. I told them that God's peace only comes from having a relationship with His son, Jesus Christ. Jesus says in John 14:27, "Peace I leave you with, my peace I give to you, not as the world gives do I give to you, let not your heart be troubled neither let it be afraid." I explained to them the peace of God that came upon us in the midst of this accident. They both had smiles on their faces and agreed to what was said.

After sharing with them and talking about the job, they wished my wife and me well, and they departed. After they left, I mentioned to my wife that each time my co-worker came down from Toledo, Ohio; I had the opportunity to share my relationship with Jesus Christ with him. My co-worker had mentioned to me that he didn't grow up in the church, but he did attend Church from time to time.

We could never assume how God is working in someone's heart to bring them into having a relationship with Him. I do know that our lifestyle must reflect the love of Christ so that others may see that Christ lives within us. I remember when my co-worker and others from Toledo, Ohio, questioned me about sharing my faith with others on the job.

A gentleman I was working with complained to my supervisor that I was always talking about religion to him and other co-workers. He was upset during that time, so someone called our main office in Toledo, Ohio, and word got to my supervisors and others about my conversation on my faith. They called a special meeting that evening to have a video conference. The Conference was held by my supervisor and three others from Toledo, Ohio. They wanted to know if the workers wanted to keep me as their Transportation supervisor. My co-worker was offended, so they called him in without my presence and spoke to him about me sharing my religion with him and others. I don't know what was said, as they kept him in the conference for about an hour and a half. They called me in to speak to me about what was shared with them by my co-worker. The first thing they told me about was why they called this conference. They stated that they understood that I was a religious person, but while on the job, my religious conversations must not be shared with other co-workers. They shared how it offended others, but I knew who they were talking about. They went over my duty assignments of all my responsibilities as a Transportation supervisor.

All those who led this conference were in agreement that I must not share my religion with any of my co-workers. After they explained what I couldn't do and what I was supposed to be doing, they asked me if I had any questions or comments.

At that time, I had a hat on my head that I had brought to the conference. Truly this was only by the power of the holy spirit that gave me the words to share at this conference. I told them that I appreciated all that was said to me. My statement, as I told them, was that I first don't just have a religion, but I have a relationship with Jesus Christ. I also shared with them that I, too, have two hats that I wear at this job. I raised the hat I was wearing and shared with them that on the side of the hat, I have a responsibility to be a transportation supervisor for all the drivers under my care. I then turned my hat around and stated that I also have a responsibility to share my relationship with others and to have the desire to hear what God has for me to share.

I honestly have to say that when the opportunity arises, I just can't say I would not share who I am in Christ as I serve a living God. In the Book of Romans 1:16, Paul stated, "We are not to be ashamed of the gospel of Christ, for it is the power of God unto salvation for everyone who believes."

After sharing what I had to say to those at this conference, you could practically hear a pin drop, as it was so quiet in that place. I knew God gave me those words to say by the power of the Holy Spirit. This was truly an opportunity to bring glory to God and not to me. After I had finished, these individuals at the conference stated, "We truly like the work you are doing as a Transportation Supervisor, and we would like to keep you in that position. Please remember why we hired you and not to share so much about your religion." I thanked them and put a smile on my face as this was the end of the conversation.

It's amazing that after a few days, my co-worker wouldn't say much to me. I was just praying for him, but I sensed my co-worker had some guilty feelings. He came to me one day and stated that he apologized for what he did by calling Toledo, Ohio, about me sharing my faith. I told him that it was no harm done, so I didn't have any feelings against him, and after that, we had a good conversation. My co-worker started asking me how I came to know Jesus Christ as my Lord and Savior. He asked me about my family, so all that happened was done for the purpose of bringing glory to God.

I know God has a purpose and plan for everything in our life. That's why it's important that we grow in grace and knowledge of our Lord and Savior, Jesus Christ. It's also important that we stay in God's word and read it daily so that it will be a lamp upon our feet and a light on our path.

The same evening after my co-workers left our home, my wife had some of her co-workers from her work that brought some more food for us to eat. This individual that brought the food over works with my wife in the office, and she also brought along her husband and their two children. I was sitting in the living room at this time with my legs propped up to elevate them. My wife brought them into the living room to introduce me to them, and we started discussing how God had kept us from this severe accident that happened to us. We spoke about the goodness of God, and they also mentioned that they attended Church as well. Meeting them was a pleasure as we spoke about God's goodness in our lives. They left after a while, but I started feeling tired after being up for so long.

I had to use my walker to get to the bedroom so that I could lie down in bed. The pain was really kicking in, so I had to eat something and take some pain medicine before I went to bed. That night I did a lot of tossing and turning, as the pain was so overwhelming throughout the night. I think I overdid it by staying up too long throughout the day. It really seemed like the medicine wasn't doing anything for the pain in my leg. I prayed that God would ease the pain and help me to rest throughout the night. My wife saw that I was struggling throughout the night, so she got up to give me some ice and placed it on my legs. The pain finally eased up, and I was able to get a little rest throughout the night.

The next day, that afternoon, we got a knock at the door

from our next-door neighbor. I was in the bedroom at the time, but my wife came in to inform me that our neighbor had come over to check on us. I got myself together and went into the living room with my walker. The first thing our neighbor said was, "I do apologize because I didn't know that you guys were in such a serious accident." Our neighbor heard about our accident from another neighbor who told her about our situation. She didn't know all the details of our accident, so we explained all that had happened; she actually works at a hospital and sees many of these tragic accidents. She commented that she was so thankful to God that He kept us alive, and of course, we agreed.

After we had finished talking about our accident and giving her the details of what happened, our neighbor suggested that she wanted to do something for us. She stated that the least she could do was help us pay one of our bills. My wife and I looked at one another with amazement, but we knew that it was God to place that desire upon her heart. She didn't specifically say which bill to pay, so I mentioned to her that our mortgage needed to be paid. She laughed, as we all laughed, because she wasn't talking about such a big bill to pay. I stated that she mentioned a bill, so why not let it be our mortgage? Then she suggested if we had a car note, and I stated that we did. This was truly a blessing that she took our information for our car payment and paid it for that month. My wife and I thanked her and told her that we really appreciated her being obedient to God, even though she wanted to do more at that time.

My mom had just witnessed this, and she also was overwhelmed by the kindness of our neighbor. This was truly a blessing to us. We saw how God was meeting and supplying all of our needs each and every day. This was also a testimony of God's faithfulness, as my Mom was there to see the goodness of God. She witnessed many of our friends and church family bringing food to feed us. This was all God making provision for us in our time of need. We were truly grateful for my mom being there, as she was such a tremendous help to my wife and I.

I can honestly say that while she was there, I probably gained at least 5 to 8 lbs eating all that good food. The time was now coming near when my mom would be going back to her home in Baltimore. I know she wanted to stay longer, but she still had my father and other family members to take care of back home.

When my Mom stayed with us, her younger brother, who lived here in Georgia, got very sick. He was taken to the hospital, but they weren't sure what had happened to him. I don't remember all the details, but it wasn't long before her brother passed away while she was still here with us.

My Mom also had another brother that lived here as well. They both went to the hospital to see my uncle, but he had passed away before they arrived. This was truly hard for my mom, especially since she was about to take the journey back to Baltimore. Even though this seemed like a sad occasion, it was God letting us all know that it was my uncle's time to depart from this world. He was a believer in Christ, so he was no longer in pain or experiencing any more suffering.

God calls His children who experience death precious; Psalms 116:15 states, "Precious in the sight of the Lord is the death of his Saints." What an awesome statement, as those that are in Christ will experience eternal life with God. For those who don't accept Jesus as their Lord and Savior, they will experience eternal damnation. Those who don't accept Jesus Christ will be separated from God eternally, as they won't have another chance once they depart from this world.

After everything settled down and all the arrangements were made for my uncle, my mom was getting ready to depart for her journey back to Baltimore. My son was going to take my mom to the airport, and I was truly thankful, along with my wife, for my Mom being able to come down and take care of us. I prayed with her, asking God to comfort her as she was still grieving over her brother's death. My wife and my mom all shared some tears about her leaving and about my uncle's death.

It was truly a blessing that God had allowed my mom to be here for us and spend time with her brother before his transition. What a mighty God we serve, as He knows everything that happens in our lives.

My mom called to let us know she had arrived safely back in Baltimore that evening. I had to hold back some tears on the phone because I was already missing her. My wife and I thanked her again for all she did for us, especially for taking the time to take care of us in our time of need.

The next day, as God awakened us to see another beautiful day, my wife and I realized how much of a blessing it had been having Mom around to help us out. My wife, now with her one arm in a sling, had to do for both of us. Our day started with prayer and reading God's Word together. I understood that God would not put any more on us than we could bear, especially since my wife was still in recovery, as I was as well. My wife didn't have to clean the house, as my mom did that before she left. The greatest challenge my wife had was trying to help me take a shower, especially since I had to use a walker to get around.

It's amazing that with that one arm, God gave my wife the strength to help me get up and get into the shower. I couldn't reach certain parts of my body due to being unable to bend down. I can truly see that my wife was a woman who honored her vows when they said in sickness and in health. This was truly the love of Christ being seen through my wife, knowing she could do all things through Christ who strengthens her. I thank God for giving me a woman who's faithful to her role as a wife, but most importantly, she was faithful to God. For we know that He gets all the glory and all the praise because of who He is in our life. After my wife had finished helping me take a shower, she then prepared breakfast for us both.

My physical therapist came over that morning to help me with some more of my exercises. We went into our living room, where the area was bigger for me to exercise more. She had me do some more leg stretching, and she also measured my leg again. I was just praising God for how much improvement my leg has overcome from the therapist working with me. The therapist was rough on me, but she knew what she was doing. My knee measurement was almost about twenty degrees, which was a lot of progress that was being made. She even had me try to walk without the walker.

I took a few steps, and then she had me try to walk up the stairs. She followed behind me, but I couldn't imagine walking up the stairs. I actually made it all the way up to the top of the stairs, but I was truly exhausted. This was truly God giving me the strength to achieve this. I was overjoyed, and of course, my wife recorded this for me. Afterward, the physical therapist helped me come back down the steps, which was a great challenge. She then allowed me to sit down and rest for a minute, then took my knee measurement again. It's amazing that walking up those steps enabled me to stretch my leg a little more. The measurement was now extended to almost thirty degrees, which was truly a blessing. The therapist then finished up and gave me some more exercises to do while I was resting in bed.

My wife came into the room to see me and asked if I wanted to go and lie down, but I was so exhausted that I went to sleep on the couch. That evening after taking a nap, my wife had a cousin that arrived, and I also had a cousin that came to visit almost at the same time. They expressed concern about how we were doing as they entered our home.

My wife and I explained to them about our accident, and all that was involved. It's amazing how both of them cleaned the house and went into the kitchen to help my wife put some dinner together. I was so overjoyed at how they just stepped in and worked like it was their own house to clean up. My wife could sit down and relax as they told her to allow them to help as much as they could. This was the first time my wife could sit down and relax with that arm in a sling since my mom left to return to Baltimore. After they had finished cleaning the house, we had a chance to sit down that evening together to eat a great meal, but our conversation was even greater as we had a chance to talk about the goodness of the Lord.

It was such a blessing to share with them how God was there in the midst of our accident. Not only is God our protector, but He is also our provider as well. He knows our needs even before we petition them in prayer, as each of us could share how well God was working in our individual lives. We started praising and worshiping the Lord, as it was such an awesome time we had together that evening.

We finish eating and talking about the goodness of God. My wife's cousin left that evening, but my cousin decided to stay overnight and help even more the next day. This had truly been a full day for me, so I had to use my walker to go back to the bedroom to get ready for bed. I had to take some pain medicine, as I was in a lot of pain from staying up most of the day. The next day we all were awakened early, as my cousin was up fixing breakfast for us. This was truly a blessing for my wife and me, especially since my wife was able to get some more rest. After we ate breakfast, we then started talking about the Lord again. I asked my cousin if she wanted to have Bible study, and she was delighted to have Bible study with us.

We did a Bible study about memorizing scripture, as this helps us in our walk with the Lord. I was familiar with this study because we used to have Bible study in our home with some neighbors. I went over a few scriptures that most people often memorize, like John 3:16: "For God so loved the world that he gave his only begotten son that whosoever believes in him shall not perish but have everlasting life." The main thing about this lesson was memorizing God's word so that the

Holy Spirit could work in us and bring back to our memory what God says from his Word. We had an awesome discussion, and an example of scripture was given to us from the book of Joshua 1:9. Joshua was now given the assignment to lead the children of Israel to the promised land. His mentor Moses was no longer with him, and the people were accustomed to hearing from God through His servant, Moses. What an assignment Joshua now had, to not only hear from God but also to relay what He said from His word. Joshua stated that we must meditate on His word day and night.

My cousin really enjoyed this lesson because she stated that she didn't have one-on-one time with others to study God's word. We didn't realize how much time had passed by, but it was a little past noon. My cousin's husband had just arrived to come to pick her up. We really enjoyed having my cousin spend this time with us, especially since we were able to get into God's word.

We prayed together, and we told her how much we appreciated her time to clean up and cook for us as well. When she left, my wife and I had some more conversations about the Lord. We were so thankful for all that God was doing in our life. God was truly working in my wife and I, as we had more time to spend together talking and reading His Word. It's amazing how we take how much time we have together as married couples for granted. Life can be so busy, with working, cleaning, watching TV, and doing so many other busy things.

God was showing us how to prioritize time to spend together with one another. The enemy can be so suttled with a married couple that they can go through life not riealizing how much time has gone by being so busy. I was learning more about my wife and seeing how much I really appreciated her. God ordained us to be as one, and that involved in sickness and good health. I can truly say that God has blessed me with a virtuous wife who takes care of her household as well. Proverbs 31:27a states, "She watches over the ways of her household." I Praise God for having someone who has a heart for His Word and lives according to His Word as well. According to James 1:22–24, "We must be doers of the Word and not hearers only deceiving ourselves. For if anyone is a hearer of the Word and not a doer, he is like a man observing his natural face in the mirror. For he observes himself, goes away and immediately forgets what kind of man he was."

I actually saw my wife being a doer of God's Word and putting it into practice. It amazes me how many followers of Christ today are not doers of God's Holy Word. Many people go to church, but outside the church, their lifestyle is different from day-to-day activities. I know from reading God's word that Paul the Apostle struggled with living in the flesh as well. Galatians 5:16–17 states, "I say then walk in the spirit, and you should not fulfill the lust of the flesh. For the flesh lusts against the spirit and the spirit against the flesh, and these are contrary to one another so that you do not do the things that you wish." This is truly an example given by Paul of how many followers of Christ today struggle with how to obey the Holy Spirit that dwells within them.

The Holy Spirit was given to all believers in Christ to lead and guide them into all truth. He reminds us of all Christ has done for us; I know that when I think about the price that Jesus paid for me; He took my sin and nailed it to the cross. Romans 6:8 states: "But God demonstrated His own love toward us, in that while we were still sinners Christ died for us."

Christ had me in mind while He was dying on the cross. He already knew that one day, I would recognize the need for a Savior in my life. I truly thank God for my salvation, knowing I couldn't save myself. It is only by God's grace and His love that He has shown us through the death of His Son that God is good. Knowing what God has done for me gives me hope of knowing that one day I will be able to run again.

The therapist that had been coming to our home came over for one last visit on a Friday morning. She took out her chart and showed me the progress we had made during her few visits with me. She mentioned that she was impressed with how far I had come trying to walk and exercise my leg. We did some more exercises that day, and she also helped me walk around the house and take a few steps without the walker. She did her final measurement, which was a little over thirty degrees. Now that she had finished her sessions with me, she gave me some numbers to call for in-person visits to a therapist's office.

    I now needed to do more exercises that she didn't have access to, like trying to pedal on a stationary bike. I appreciated her and all that she had done for me. My wife also told her that she appreciated her hard work and patience with me. After she left, my wife went to check the mail, and we had received a bill from the hospital. We started receiving so many medical bills from the hospital, along with the Ambulance Company as well; my wife was getting really concerned about how we were going to pay these bills. We contacted the lawyer, and they just told us to fax the bills over to their office. Every bill that came in we would be responsible for until the settlement was final. This was a big concern for my wife, but I just told her that God knows our needs and will continue to meet and supply all of our needs.

    But God knows our needs even before we ask, so He reminds us in Matthew 6:33 to "seek ye first the kingdom of God and His righteousness and everything else will be added unto you." Not only did we receive these medical bills, but we were still receiving our own personal bills as well. It was about this time now that I wasn't receiving any more paychecks from my job. The last check I received, we could take care of the bills that particular week.

    We were also about to approach another month that we had to pay our mortgage and other bills. We were receiving short-term disability pay for my wife, but at this time, no pay was coming in for me. This was really starting to concern me, as my wife wanted to know how we would manage without enough income coming in. As I told her before, and reminded her again, God is faithful. I was trying to encourage my wife to trust God and believe in His Word. This was really starting to be a great challenge for me, but I wouldn't allow my wife to see it through me as well.

I started reading God's Word again, but I couldn't even concentrate or stay focused on what I was reading. My mind was so absorbed with so much about our bills and concentrated on not being able to run or walk again. I was concerned about how I could, in my position, take care of my household. I wasn't in any position to go out and get a job to make money. All these thoughts were crowding my mind, and this truly wasn't easy to overcome.

That afternoon, I received an encouraging call from my pastor to check on us. I didn't discuss with him all that I was going through, but as we talked for a few minutes, my pastor realized that I needed some prayer. Not only did he pray with me, but he also encouraged me to stay faithful to God and continue reading His Word. I just started shedding some tears because that's what I needed at that moment. It's just so great to know that we serve a God that knows what we need in our times of weariness or distress. My pastor also asked if we needed anything and how we were doing. I told him it had been a challenge, but I appreciated his calling and praying with me that day.

After our conversation ended, I told my wife that our pastor had called and given me some encouraging words. At this moment, I was able to mention to my wife how I was struggling with our bills, and not enough money was coming in. The Holy Spirit convicted me for not sharing this with her. I really didn't want to share this with her, as my pride was getting the best of me, not wanting me to share.

Once I shared this with her, we discussed even more about what to do. We both concluded that only God could handle this situation. We both bowed before the Lord and started weeping and praying to our God, who is faithful. We were confessing any wrongdoings that we've committed against God and his Word and realized that we were not walking by faith and trusting in God, who is able to meet and supply all of our needs. We were trying to figure out what we could do to pay our bills ourselves. I believe this is the way most Christians view life situations on a day-to-day basis. We have to figure something out rather than trusting in our God, who is able to meet and supply all of our needs. God tells us in His Word to cast all of our cares upon Him because He cares for us, according to 1 Peter 5:7.

Even though the situation was still before us, we realized that this had to be the work of God. I do believe, for that moment, that we had such a peace that surpassed all understanding that God had given us. The same day, I also called to find a place to go for my physical therapy on my leg. We found a place not too far from home, about ten minutes away. They wanted me to come in for a consultation and also to verify our insurance.

I was sharing with my wife that the young lady I spoke with really had compassion about my situation. I felt comfortable about going to this place even though I hadn't yet seen it. They wanted to know if I could come in the next day, so I checked with my wife, and she didn't have any appointments. I was excited about going to this place to help me with my leg and strengthen it. After we settled down and went to bed, I had another rough night trying to get comfortable, seeing that I was in a lot of pain.

When we woke in the morning, we started by giving thanks to God for another glorious day. I told my wife that I didn't get much rest the previous night because I was in a lot of pain. The appointment with the therapist was that morning, so I told my wife that I still wanted to attend. It was a great challenge trying to get me into the car, but by God's grace, we managed. We arrived at the place, and my wife struggled with that one arm to help me get out of the car. Once we got inside, I was able to be seen by the therapist in charge. We went over what their goals were and how they could help me get to my goals as well. They stated that they would need to see me at least three times a week to help me with my progress. I told them this was fine, but they had to check with my insurance first. The secretary called and found out this was okay, but we would have to pay a $25 co-pay for each visit. I explained to them that I wasn't getting paid from my job, so this would not work out, coming at least three times a week. They asked me what I could afford, so I again explained to them about not having any money, but we had an attorney working on our case. I suggested to maybe only see them twice a week instead of three times. They stated that it's important that they see me at least three times a week, so they were willing to work with me on how we could pay.

 I didn't know how God would work this out, but they went in the back and came back with a decision. God had placed upon their hearts to make a way for me to come in three times a week and not to worry about my co-pay, which was $25 for each visit. I saw God working for the good, for those who love Him and for those who are called according to His purpose. They scheduled me that next Monday, and I would come in each week on Monday, Wednesday and Friday. The weekend came, and this was the first weekend that my wife and I didn't have anyone to visit us. We did have some people call and check in with us, and I also received a call from my uncle to check in with us to see how we were doing. He also wanted to know our address as he wanted to give us something. I asked him why he wanted our address, as I thought he wanted to send us some money. I always thought my uncle had a lot of money because he dressed well and had nice vehicles to drive. He actually wanted our address because, to our surprise, the following week, my uncle sent to our home two young ladies to clean our home. This was truly a blessing that we were not expecting, for these young ladies to come and clean our whole house. These ladies did a wonderful job, and my wife was truly pleased with how they cleaned our home. I know this was a true blessing for my wife, especially since she didn't have to clean the house with her one arm.

We called my uncle, and we told him how much we really appreciated such a blessing from the Lord that he had done for us.

He stated that the Lord had placed this upon his heart, so he was obedient to follow through. We don't know how much he paid these ladies, but we only had a few dollars around the house to give them a tip for their time cleaning our home. They finished that afternoon, and it was right on time as I had to attend my first therapy appointment around 1:00 pm.

My wife helped me to get dressed and into the car. I'm just so amazed as to how my wife was such a blessing to me in this time of need. Once we arrived and I checked in, they took me to the back, as I was using some crutches. We went to this room so they could do the measurement on my leg, as the therapist had done at my house. The measurement was about twenty degrees, that I could stretch out my leg. I told him I could get it up to thirty degrees when I left my last meeting appointment with my in-house therapist. They made a note and told me their goal was to get me to at least sixty degrees before they finished with me.

We started doing some different leg exercises, and each one was a challenge. They even tried to help me walk without my crutches, which was an even greater challenge. After we were done, I was in a lot of pain and wanted some pain medicine. They measured my leg again, and it was now about twenty-five degrees. I came out to see my wife, and she told me that they would also set up some appointments to help her with her arm. I was now wondering how we would pay not only for my visit but for her visit as well. We had the same insurance, so she also would have to make a $25 co-payment. They set up her visits to be the same day as mine due to her having to bring me to my appointments. They also mentioned that they would continue to work out what was needed to be paid for each one of our visits. It amazes me how God works things out in our lives, yet we still question how things will work out.

I know for most Christians, as we follow Christ, we move by sight instead of walking by faith. God says in Hebrews 11:6, "But without faith it is impossible to please Him for he who comes to God must believe that He is and that He is a rewarder of those who diligently seek Him." God desires for us to trust Him and obey His Word. I was now struggling with how we would be able to make payments for both of our visits since we would be coming in at the same time.

We left the clinic, and my wife was excited that she would also be doing some physical therapy for her arm. I didn't mention to her how we would pay for both of our visits, especially since she couldn't wait to get started on her arm and shoulder. At this time, my wife was still wearing a sling on her shoulder to support her arm. I know sometimes my wife was in pain, but despite her pain, she helped me get through my appointments.

That evening when we arrived home, my wife checked the mail. We were still getting some hospital bills that I knew we couldn't even try to pay due to not enough money coming into our household. My wife called the attorney representing us, and they told her to fax them over to their office. They also told her that nothing could be done at this time until the settlement came in. My wife also called our insurance company, as they were making payments for the medical bills, but we also had to pay our deductibles. This was truly a time when we had so many bills coming in and not enough income to pay even our personal bills.

Our mortgage was coming due next month, and my wife

was asking me if we would be able to make the payment. She already knew that I wasn't getting paid from my job, so I just told her that everything would be okay. We'll trust God and see how He works things out for us. I was still in a lot of pain, so my wife fixed something to eat, and I was able to take some pain medicine. That appointment with the therapist really wore me out, so I told my wife that I just wanted to relax. We went to bed kind of early that night, and we did pray together about our financial situation.

5

How Do We Handle One Struggle After Another?

The next morning as we were awakened, my wife was ready to go and cook us some breakfast. I received a call that morning from my job; from a gentleman that was in a high position in our company. He asked me how my wife and I were doing. I believe he was truly concerned. I told him about us going through physical therapy and how things were going with that. He then asked me how we were doing financially. I told him that I was not getting paid by his company at that time. He stated that he'd talked with the company's owners, and they mentioned that they really appreciated the quality of my work in their business. This gentleman said to me that they decided to continue to pay me my regular salary every week until I could come back to work. I was a weekly salary employee since I was their Transportation Manager. My wife was there listening, and I was just speechless! Tears were rolling down my face, and all I could say with so many tears flowing was, "Thank You"! He stated that he had already worked it out with payroll to continue having my checks directly deposited each week. I was so overwhelmed with gratitude that I told him to thank the owners.

The conversation ended with this gentleman, and my wife and I just started praising God! I just saw how God worked in the hearts of this company's owners to ensure that our needs were being taken care of. What an awesome God we serve, knowing that He supplies all of our needs according to His riches in Glory by Christ Jesus. We had no idea that God was working behind the scenes, ensuring that our needs were being met. I wasn't able to get up and go to work due to this accident with a broken femur.

God makes a way for us in the midst of our trials and tribulations. His desire for us, as His children, is to trust Him with all of our hearts and not lean toward our own understanding. God's word reminds us that He will never leave us, nor will He forsake us. We serve a God that knows our needs even before we ask. I told my wife that this was truly a testimony. Romans 8:28 states, "God works all things together for the good, for those who love Him and for those who are called according to His purpose." This is a familiar scripture that many believers in the body of Christ are aware of. God loves all His children, and He will continue to make provision for those who will trust Him and obey His commands.

I had no idea God was working things out for our good, especially since we had limited income. In most cases, we try to help God by going out to get another job or trying other means to pay the bills that are due. This was a different situation, as we had to depend totally on God to supply what we needed in our immediate situation. I believe this is how faith works, that we must depend totally upon God and come to the understanding that He is Sovereign over all. This means that God is in control, and He knows what's best for our present situation. This was truly a testimony that my wife and I wanted to share with many about how God is faithful to His Word!

That day, as my wife spoke to others who had called and checked on us, I could hear her conversation about sharing how God had made a way about our financial situation. I had also spoken to my older brother, who lives in Baltimore, and shared with him about the goodness of God. He called that day to check on us, and I was so excited that I had to share what God had done on our behalf. My brother was also excited as I shared what my job had done for us. He also asked me how I was doing since the accident. This was the first conversation I had with my brother since the accident, as I shared with him what happened in our situation and how the accident happened. He also asked me if I needed anything, so I told him we were doing fine.

My brother and his wife at this time were doing well financially, so I believe he was offering money if we needed any. I still had to wait to get my first check deposit from the company, so we still needed help financially.

Once again, I had allowed my pride to get in the way by saying that everything was okay with us financially. Before I finished talking with my brother, we said a prayer, and our conversation ended. The next day, as my wife and I were awakened, we started our day with prayer and time in His Holy Word. We were both still thankful that God had worked things out for our financial situation. Even though I would start getting paid from my job this coming Friday, we still had bills to be caught up on, along with our mortgage that was due next month. After we finished with our morning devotion in God's Word, my wife went to cook us some breakfast to get our day started. We didn't have anything on our schedule for this day, so we just relaxed around the house and enjoyed one another's company. I'm just so grateful for how God was drawing my wife and me closer together. I know sometimes my wife probably felt like I was getting on her nerves, but God was showing us how to have patience with one another. Spending a lot of time with one another can be challenging, but I realized we needed to depend on one another.

I had to depend more on my wife, so God was working on me to have more patience and to appreciate her even more.

It's amazing how most people in a marriage relationship don't appreciate one another but take their spouse for granted. A husband stops buying flowers for his wife or taking her out on a date and having small conversations. A wife stops giving her husband compliments about how she appreciates all he does as a provider. Even though these are just little things to do with one another, little things in life can be much appreciated. I believe that's how we ought to be with our walk with God, to really appreciate everything that He does in our life.

Each day that He awakens us is truly a blessing to give thanks because He is the one that breathes the breath of life in us. Psalms 100:3 says, "Know that the Lord, He is God, and it is He who has made us and not we ourselves, we are His people and the sheep of His pasture." It just amazes me how so many people in this life don't appreciate or realize that we serve a true and living God. So as we went throughout this day, we did have a few people that called to check up on us. My wife was receiving more calls coming in to her than I was. She was spending more time on the phone, so I felt a little jealous at times. I wasn't receiving many calls from some of the brothers that were part of our church. I felt lonely sometimes because I didn't have another brother to share my feelings with. I share some things with my wife, but it's nothing like sharing with another brother about what you're going through. I did have a few brothers that called from the church, but I guess some brothers thought they were bothering me. I just needed that brotherly love from those who have a close relationship with the Lord for the encouragement I needed at this particular time.

I truly thank God for our Church family, who always pray for us. To our surprise, we had a visit from our pastor and his wife on this day. They came over to encourage us and to have communion with us as well. Our pastor gave us a lesson about why we partake of the Communion, and he also spoke about the two elements (bread and wine). We were truly blessed by this visit from our pastor and his wife as a reminder of what Christ did for us and the ultimate price He paid for our sins. This was truly needed by both of us to have prayer and communion with our pastor and his wife. I know our pastor would have stayed a little longer and given more teaching to us, but he doesn't believe in staying long when he comes to visit the sick. This was one of the lessons our pastor wanted to teach us as leaders in the Church.

I can honestly say that our pastor and his wife love God's people, and they love to minister to others about being faithful to God. They were two examples of how one is faithful to the ministry. Not only do we have a pastor that teaches well, but he is also a true example of a follower of Christ. Our pastor always points God's people to Jesus and His Word. He never puts any emphasis on himself, but he always shares that it's not about him, but always to bring glory to God and to put Him on display. Paul says in Galatians 2:20, "I have been crucified with Christ and it is no longer I who live but Christ lives in me and the life I now live in the flesh I live by faith in the Son of God who loved me and gave Himself for me."

I do believe that once we have accepted Jesus Christ as our Lord and Savior; we become new creatures in Christ. Our old lifestyle was centered around all that we could do, which is how we lived before entering an intimate relationship with Jesus Christ. I know for me that I was recognizing and appreciating all that Jesus has done as He went to the cross to be crucified on our behalf. Crucifixion was a lot of pain, as Christ took our punishment to become sin on our behalf. It was God who allowed the punishment of our sin to be placed upon his only begotten Son. Isaiah 53:4–5 states, "Surely He has borne our griefs and carried our sorrows, yet we esteemed Him smitten by God and afflicted, but He was wounded for our transgressions, He was bruised for our iniquities, the chastisement for our peace was upon Him, and by His stripes we are healed."

I thank God that He had me in mind when He sent His son to be Savior for those whom He has chosen before the foundation of the world. Because God is omniscient, which means He is all-knowing, He is the one who allowed my wife and I to go through what we went through during this tragic accident. It is truly amazing how I can look back and see how God was working things out on our behalf. When you're actually going through a trial or tribulation, it's difficult to say, "I trust God," because we don't see immediate results.

Since God is the one who created the world and everything in it, I want to know why most believers claim that they follow Jesus but can't trust God for everything. God spoke to the owner of this company I work for to keep me on payroll weekly. I truly didn't think or know how God would work it out for our bills to be paid. We just had to trust God totally and believe in what He says in His Holy Word. Romans 10:17 says, "Faith comes by hearing and hearing by the Word of God."

Our faith is strengthened as we read and meditate on God's Word daily! This is why so many people struggle with trusting God, because they don't spend enough time in His Word to get to know Him for who He is. God knew that we were coming to the end of this month and that our mortgage would be due along with all the other obligations that we had. My wife was still being persistent in asking me about what we were going to do as the time was drawing near to pay our mortgage. I had so much on my mind and was also dealing with the pain in my leg as well. There were times when I was reading God's Word, and I would get frustrated because I had several things going on at one time in my mind. God had just opened up a financial blessing for us, as I received the call from my job about getting paid weekly. It's like we come out of one crisis and then it's another one just waiting at the door. God says that He is the same God yesterday, today, and forever more.

If I believe that God provided for us and made a resource to continue to pay our bills, then why am I struggling with this situation about our mortgage being paid? This was on my mind most of the day, and I even went to bed with those thoughts on my mind. I couldn't rest throughout the night, especially since the pain in my leg was keeping me awake as well. My wife saw that I was having a rough night, so she got up and asked me how I was doing. I told her that the pain in my leg was keeping me awake and I needed to take some pain medicine. I did take some pain medication, and my wife also went to get me a sandwich to help me with the medicine so that I wouldn't get nauseous. My wife noticed that I was a little quiet, so she asked me what was on my mind. It's like she could read my face and noticed that I had something on my mind. I finally shared with her that our mortgage payment was due soon, and I really trusted that God would make a way. I just didn't know how this would happen since we didn't have enough money to pay our mortgage.

My wife reminded me that God is in control, and He knows the situation at hand. He hasn't forgotten us, and He would not forsake us! I needed to hear that, as I always was there to encourage my wife about the faithfulness of God. God was using my wife to remind me that I must trust in Him and not grow weary. After we finished talking about how we must trust God, we then said a prayer together. I felt better and was able to get some rest throughout the night.

The next day we both had to go to our physical therapy appointment. I still struggled to get into the car, as my wife had to help me with her one arm. She finally got me into the car, and I was now exhausted and in a lot of pain.

I was praying that the Lord would give us the strength to be able to make our appointment to see the therapist to help both of us. Once we arrived, my wife helped me out of the car. We got inside and noticed how crowded it was.

We were waiting in the area to be checked in, and I noticed a gentleman that looked familiar to me. He was sitting a few chairs away from me, so I asked him if he was ever in the military. He stated that he had just finished his time serving in the Army and was hurt while he was finishing up his last tour. We had a great conversation about the military, but it turned out that I didn't know him after all. I was able to share with him about how God has kept my wife and me in our accident. I told him that God continues to provide and meet all of our needs in the midst of what happened after our accident. He also mentioned that he was blessed, as God kept him while he was serving in the military. He had injured his leg and was going through physical therapy, as I was as well. This gentleman was very tall, and I assumed that he played basketball.

As it happens, he did mention that he used to play basketball before he left to go into the service. We had a great conversation about his time in the service and about the goodness of God. I didn't get a chance to ask him if he had a relationship with Jesus Christ because I was called to go into the back to start my physical therapy appointment. My wife was also called right after me, as they were working on her shoulder and right arm as well. We both had a good workout, and they did another measurement on my leg to see the progress. My leg measured at thirty-five degrees, which was a good sign of some motion improvement.

After we were done and went to check out to pay our deductible, the young lady at the checkout desk stated that we didn't have to pay any more deductibles. I looked at my wife strangely, and she looked at me as if I had paid them in advance. The young lady at the desk stated that we had met our deductible for the year and no more co-payments were needed for our visits. My wife and I just started praising God and informing others in that place of how good and awesome God is. I didn't see the other gentleman to share with him about what God had done, as he probably was in the back doing his physical therapy.

Once my wife and I got back into the car and my wife was able to get me situated, we started praising God even more before we left our appointment. We left and arrived home, and we both were exhausted from working out at our physical therapy appointment.

It took my wife a while to help me out of the car, as she was in pain with her arm again. It was hard to get me out of the car, but we finally got situated and got into the house. My wife then went to check the mail, and we once again had some bills that we had to pay from the accident. We were rejoicing at the therapy office when we got the information about not having to pay any more of our co-payments; now, we were exhausted and tired and seeing more of these medical bills.

We once again were discouraged about not having enough money to pay these bills on time. It's just amazing how our walk of life with the Lord can be up one minute and then down another. I know we were praising God for what happened at the therapy office, as we just were so excited that we couldn't help but share with others. I was very tired, and when my wife showed me these extra bills that we had to pay from the accident that wasn't our fault, I got a little frustrated. I just wanted to get some rest and forget about all these bills that I had just seen; knowing that they wouldn't go away by going to sleep because they were real and wouldn't just disappear.

I believe that's how most believers today face their own issues, as they would love for their problems to just go away immediately. When we face issues or problems that are out of our control, these are times when God wants us to trust Him so that we don't lean on our own understanding. These bills that we were facing were truly out of our control, and that week we also were coming up to pay our home mortgage. As the end of the week approached, I received my pay from the company I worked for. With the amount I received from my company that week and the money my wife received, we were able to catch up on some of our bills. I was the one that normally paid our bills, so I knew that we only had enough just to play catch up. Since this was the end of the month and our mortgage was due, as well as all the other bills, I knew we didn't have enough to pay the mortgage that month. I really didn't know where or how this was going to happen, but I was praising God for what He had already done by playing catch up for some of the other bills. It's amazing how in most marriages, when it comes to bills and finances, these are limited discussions. I normally don't discuss with my wife what's paid out and how much is left in our account. It's like she just trusts that I'm paying all the bills on time.

I realize it's been that way in our marriage for years, and I'm not sure why it's been like that. I needed to share with her that it's been a struggle since we have been in this situation since the accident. I know that God was working on me to share more about our financial obligations to my wife so that we could pray together. It was just so awesome how God was drawing us closer to trust and communicate more with one another.

There are so many of what I call "barriers" in the marriage, where couples don't spend enough time discussing issues they face together. For God ordained us to be as One in the beginning, and this is how we are to operate in our relationship. Spending quality time together and growing in His Word helps us to build each other up and grow strong in the Lord and in the power of His might. I do know that we have so many challenges that we face as a couple, and we try to rely upon ourselves instead of relying on and trusting God in His Word.

In most cases we try to make decisions on our own, until we come to realize that it's come to a point that it is out of our control. I had to come to the point that I couldn't do anything about what could be done to make our mortgage payment. This was a big struggle for me, as I had to trust that God could supply all of our needs, knowing that I belong to God and for what He has done for me through the finished work of Jesus. There's nothing too hard for God, and because He knows all about our needs, He is able to meet and supply every need as we ask in faith, for all things are possible to those who believe in what God says in His Word.

The next day, I received a call from our mortgage company. The call came in that morning about a conversation I had with our mortgage company around February of that year. The gentleman introduced himself and asked to speak to me and confirm my identity. After I confirmed my identity, the conversation started out to remind me of the purpose of this call. The gentleman stated that during the month of February of that year, I had started the process of refinancing my mortgage for a lower interest rate. I honestly had forgotten about this process, and the gentleman was calling to apologize for not contacting me sooner to inquire about refinancing our mortgage. He stated that I was approved to get a lower interest rate and asked if I was still interested. I told him that I was definitely interested and asked what I needed to do since this happened in February. He stated that I was already pre-approved with a lower interest rate, but he needed to send me some new documents to e-sign by way of the computer.

Once he forwarded those documents and they were sent back, I asked what the next step would be. The gentleman stated that since this was pre-approved, my mortgage payments would be lowered to a lesser monthly payment. He said I would not have to make this month's mortgage payment or for the next two months. When this was mentioned over the phone, there was a pause in our conversation. This gentleman wanted to know if I was still on the phone, as I just burst into tears. I was so overwhelmed with joy, because during this period in my walk was a big struggle to pay our mortgage on time with insufficient funds coming in. I started praising God and telling this gentleman that this was God who made all this happen in His appointed time. In the midst of me shedding tears, I was able to share with this gentleman our testimony about our accident. As I was sharing with him about the goodness of God, I could hear in his voice how the Holy Spirit was ministering to him about what was shared about our situation. After we finished our conversation, I hung up the phone and called my wife to share this good news about how God is faithful to His Word. I asked her if she remembered when I started the process of refinancing our mortgage back in February. She said she didn't remember, so I refreshed her memory as I had just received a call from our mortgage company. I told her all the details of our conversation and how God made a way that we didn't have to pay our mortgage this month along with the next two months. We both started worshiping and praising God for His faithfulness and for meeting and supplying all of our needs.

What an awesome God we serve! Who knows our needs even before we ask. Matthew 6:33-34 states, "But seek ye first the kingdom of God and His righteousness and all these things will be added unto you. Therefore, don't worry about tomorrow because tomorrow will worry about itself."

I share this testimony with many who can read about how God is on His throne and how He can strengthen and encourage His children no matter what struggles they face in this life. My prayer is that someone who reads this booklet and doesn't know God along with His son, Jesus Christ, that they will recognize that God desires all whom He has chosen will come to have a relationship with Him through His son, Jesus Christ.

In order to have a relationship with His son, Jesus Christ, one must first recognize that he or she is a sinner. Romans 3:23 says, "For all have sinned and fallen short of the glory of God." Romans 6:23 says, "For the wages of sin is death, but the gift of God is eternal life through Jesus Christ Our Lord." Once an individual has recognized that they are a sinner and also understands that there is nothing they can do to save themselves in order to have a relationship with God, Romans 5:8 says, "But God proves His own Love for us, in that while we were still sinners, Christ died for us." Ephesians 2:8 says, "For you are saved by grace through faith, and this is not from yourself; it is a gift from God, not from works so that no one could boast." The work of Salvation is for God's glory, and it is not accomplished by human works. The whole process of Salvation is not a human achievement, but it's an act of God's goodness.

One must also recognize a need for a Savior in their life as John 14:6 states, "I am the way, the truth and the life and no one comes to the Father but through me." These are the words of Jesus written by John the Apostle, who is the author that wrote these words. When one comes to that understanding from God through the power of His Holy Spirit that brings conviction to that individual. Romans 9:10–11 states, "If you confess with your mouth 'Jesus is Lord,' and believe in your heart that God has raised him from the dead, you shall be saved. With the heart one believes, resulting in righteousness and one confesses with His mouth resulting in Salvation."

I thank God with all my heart for anyone who God draws to have a relationship with Him through His Son, Jesus Christ. And now may the God of peace who brought again from the dead that great Shepherd of the sheep with the blood of the eternal covenant, even our Lord Jesus bring you peace as you enjoy this testimony. To God be the glory both now and forevermore, and no matter what you're going through, "Count It All Joy." Amen!

As of December 2022, We Praise The Lord for strengthening us both in our physical body and growing strong in the Lord. We are able to go on with our lives to do some of the daily activities we did before the accident. My wife can move her right arm well, and I can walk well. I'm not able to run anymore, but I praise God for where He's brought us from. When the weather is cold outside or rainy, we both experience some aches and stiffness with those pins that are inside my left leg and her right arm.

We also give thanks to God for working through all our financial obligations, as we didn't receive much from the lawyer we hired. Throughout the process, we actually had to file bankruptcy, but thanks be to God that we're no longer in bankruptcy.

What a joy it is for us to be here today, as The Lord has blessed us to see our grandchildren and spend quality time with them whenever time permits. I'm also grateful for God's grace and how He has strengthened our relationship to enjoy and love one another more each day.

God is faithful, and I thank God for His saving grace through His Son, Jesus Christ. Be blessed!

About Atmosphere Press

Atmosphere Press is an independent, full-service publisher for excellent books in all genres and for all audiences. Learn more about what we do at atmospherepress.com.

We encourage you to check out some of Atmosphere's latest releases, which are available at Amazon.com and via order from your local bookstore:

Finding Us, by Kristin Rehkamp

The Ideological and Political System of Banselism, by Royard Halmonet Vantion (Ancheng Wang)

Unconditional: Loving and Losing an Addict, by Lizzy and Adam

Telling Tales and Sharing Secrets, by Jackie Collins, Diana Kinared, and Sally Showalter

Nursing Homes: A Missionary's Journey Through Heaven's Waiting Room, by Tim Eatman Ph.D.

Timeline of Stars, by Joe Adcock

A Boy Who Loved Me, by Wilson Semitti

The Injustice in Justice, by Charmaine Loverin

Living in the Gray, by Katie Weber

Living with Veracity, Dying with Dignity, by Alison Clay-Duboff

Noah's Rejects, by Rob Kagan

A lot of Questions (with no answers)?, by Jordan Neben

Cowboy from Prague: An Immigrant's Pursuit of the American Dream, by Charles Ota Heller

Sleeping Under the Bridge, by Melissa Baker

The Only Prayer I Ever Have to Say Is Thank You, by M. Kaya Hill

Amygdala Blue, by Paul Lomax

About the Author

Growing up in the heart of Baltimore, Maryland, my parents would take us kids to church some Sundays and send us into the children's church. I did not quite understand what having a relationship with God was all about until I left home and joined the military.

I was a dedicated soldier in the Army which offered me the opportunity to travel and find out what I wanted to achieve. As a young man, I began to realize that I was a sinner seperated from God. I attended church service on Sunday in many of the places that the Army sent me to, and I was a leader with many responsibilities.

The Word of God was speaking to me through the ministry of The Holy Spirit. On one particular occasion, I met this gentleman who asked me a question: "Do you have a relationship with God through Jesus Christ?" I responded by stating that I did not; God was opening my eyes to realize that Jesus was the only way to the Father.

I am proud to say that I am a soldier for the Lord to share my testimony. It is by grace that I am saved.

www.ingramcontent.com/pod-product-compliance
Lightning Source LLC
LaVergne TN
LVHW041225080526
838199LV00083B/3327